SASH'S NEW HOME

By:

Loretta Cassady

Illustrated by Ren Cordova

Dedication

This book is for my daughters, Stacey & Sherry with all my love.

Acknowledgment

I would like to thank my family for always supporting me. Special thanks to my English professor, who inspired me to try my hand at writing. Thanks to Ren, my illustrator, and Benjamin for guiding me.

About the Author

Loretta Cassady is a retired RN, BSN. She lives in Kentucky with her dog, Roxie. Her previous dog was a toy poodle named Sash. She loves reading, cooking, traveling, and writing stories and books. She has been writing since college and is working on her next book.

Prologue

My name is Sasquatch, but everyone calls me Sash, which I prefer since I am a miniature, toy, black poodle. I was born on January 15th. The big name felt like more than I could handle. I'm the runt of my family, weighing about three pounds. While all of my brothers and sisters were much bigger than I, I had to fight my way to survive because I was so small.

This is the story of the ups and downs of my life. It explains how I survived and the struggles I overcame. At times, I wondered how I managed to succeed against impossible odds. It is important to keep fighting and never give up, no matter what the circumstances. You must believe in yourself before anyone else does. Stay strong and focus on what you want to achieve.

Table of Contents

Chapter One

In the early morning hours just before dawn, a whining sound could be heard throughout the house. The whining sounded like the whistling around the house on a cold, winter day. It was an ominous sound that made the hair on the back of your neck stand at attention.

Tammy, Mrs. Fear, the owner, went to investigate and found her black poodle, named Sasha, was giving birth to puppies in the corner of the laundry room. Sasha was lying in a pile of dirty clothes. Tammy was surprised because she hadn't expected Sasha to deliver her puppies this early, but it seems that Mother Nature takes its course. She watched Sasha as she delivered five tiny puppies into the cozy bed that Sasha had made for them.

They were so little, cute, and adorable. The largest pup was silver gray, just like his dad, and the next three puppies were black with silver and white spots. The last tiny puppy looked to be the runt of the litter and was solid black with a smattering of gray throughout her soft, downy coat of fur. Her eyes were black as coal with a look of longing. She was so cute, but she was so tiny compared to her brothers and sisters.

Sasha was a proud mama, and Derick, the father, was walking with his tail high in the air. He seemed to think that he had done a great job in getting these puppies here.

Derick said, "You did well, Sasha. They look like us both. Some look like you with your beautiful black coat of hair, and the others favor me with their shiny silver coat of hair. The youngest sure is small. Do you think she will make it, Sasha?"

"Yes, Derrick, I will make sure they all live. It wouldn't be pleasant if one didn't make it," Sasha declared. "I will make sure they all make it if it is the last thing I do."

As Tammy, the owner, looked down at her puppies, she wondered what she was to do with them. She thought, I will sell them when they get a little older. I believe that is what I should do when they are old enough to be weaned. It will work out fine for me, and I can make some money to boot. I hate to let them go, but I can't afford all these beautiful toy poodles. I will make sure the puppies go to wonderful homes.

Sasha heard Tammy and was saddened by the news that her puppies were going to new homes. "Derrick, what are we going to do? I can't stand to let them be taken from me. I know that is what must happen. They must go to loving homes and be companions for someone who will love each one of them. That is our purpose in life, and we must not forget that even though what we want is different," said Sasha.

Derrick stated, "I don't want to lose them either, but we will come up with something to convince Tammy to keep our family together. I believe it will be hard to lose your children because you can't watch them grow up. I know, but that is a dog's life."

Sasha said, "We have to give names to our little ones."

Derrick was ecstatic about naming his sons and daughters. Tammy, the owner, had other ideas. She said, "I will name the largest puppy with silver gray hair, Jude. I believe that fits him nicely, since he seems to root out the others. Let me think, the next one should be named Spot because he has the most white spots throughout his coat. The oldest girl puppy should be named Crista because she has silver streaks throughout her fur, which reminds me of diamonds sparkling like the sun's rays. I will call the next boy, Butch, because he looks like a fighter. Lastly, the runt of the litter is called Sasquatch because of her small size. Her coat was jet black and fluffy."

The names fit all the puppies perfectly, according to Tammy, who registered them as full-blooded toy poodles

Sasha and Derrick were not happy with the names provided by Tammy, but there was nothing they could do but accept the inevitable.

Derrick said, "I guess we will accept their names and love them all the same. Now we must convince Tammy not to sell the puppies. I have no idea how we will accomplish it."

Chapter Two

The puppies grew by leaps and bounds as the days flew by like the wind. Each one of the puppies began to show their different personality. Jude seemed to be the ruler of the bunch, and Butch lived up to his name as the fighter of the bunch. Sash just went along with the crowd, no matter what they did. Crista was the outspoken of the puppies. Sasquatch was tiny, quiet, and a shy little thing that tried to stay out of everyone's way.

Derrick and Sasha were happy with their new family. The days were filled with fun and activities for the entire family. They played hide-and-seek, rolled and ran around the house at top speed to see who could win the race. Today was a huge day for the puppies because they were six weeks old. Tammy was contemplating what to do about the poodles because her husband said he was tired of the noise, and they were always underfoot.

Tammy exclaimed, " Maybe I should advertise in the newspaper. I think that would be a great idea." She went to the newspaper office and placed an ad in the paper, "Toy Poodles for Sale." I hope someone responds to this ad quickly. I need to sell the puppies before my husband loses his cool. My husband wants the poodles sold as soon as possible. He states that they are a nuisance, but I love animals and hate to see them sold.

Derrick overheard Tammy and her husband discussing placing the puppies for sale because they couldn't afford to keep all of them. It was just too expensive to keep them all, so Tammy placed the ad to sell the poodles. He ran back to Sasha and asked, "What are we going to do? They are going to take our children away from us."

Sasha replied, "I don't know. What can we do? Remember, Derrick, that is our lot in life to be companions to people. I know we don't want to see them go, but that is our lot in life. Tammy said she would make sure they got good homes."

"I just don't know," wailed Derrick. "I trust our owners to find good homes for the puppies. They wouldn't just give them to anyone, and you know that, Derrick. You know we love our owners and trust them wholeheartedly. They have been good to us and take excellent care of us. What would we do without them to take care of us?"

Sasha replied, "Derrick, you know we love our owners and trust them wholeheartedly. They have been good to us and take excellent care of us. What would we do without them to take care of us?"

Derrick stated, "I don't know, but I guess we will have to resign ourselves to the inevitable. Our family will be split apart. I pray that each one of our children will find a good home with a loving master, which is better than winding up in the dog pound. If no one claimed our children, they would be put to sleep at the pound. Remember, Sasha, we were born to be companions to people so they could love and care for us."

Derrick agreed with Sasha that they had to abide by Tammy's rule even if they didn't want to. Both of the parents were unhappy at the thought of losing their little ones, but they knew it was probably for the best. They loved their master and wanted the same for the puppies.

Chapter Three

Some of Tammy's friends were interested in buying the toy poodles. Jude, Crista, and Spot were adopted into loving homes. They were extremely happy with their new masters.

Sasha and Derrick hated to see their babies go, but they realized it was the best for all concerned. Sasha cried and told each puppy to be happy, to enjoy, and to adapt to their new life. Derrick wished his children well and to be brave and mind their new masters. Remember, life can be a joy; you must stay positive and look for all good things in life.

Derrick said, "There will be bumps in the road, but you can overcome any problems with a strong will and common sense." He kissed each pup goodbye as they left with tears streaming down his face.

Butch and Sash were the only two puppies left of their litter. So far, no one has wanted to adopt them. A year had passed, but no one had come forward to adopt them.

Sash asked, "Why does no one want us?"

The parents replied, "I don't know, but it will happen. You must keep up a positive outlook. It will happen on its own time."

A year has passed by, and all the puppies have been sold except for Butch and Sash. Their owner, Tammy, decided to put another ad in the newspaper. She thought it might help the last two puppies find a loving and caring home. It was to the point that Tammy couldn't afford to take care of the puppies and their parents. She had a lot of birds that she was taking care of, and they were expensive. I love animals, but I have to draw the line somewhere. Tammy's husband told her that they had decided to move to Florida. That is why they had to find homes for the biggest part of their children.

Sasha overheard her master talking, and she did not like what she had heard.

"Derrick, we will be moving away from everything we know and love. Our children will be so far away from us. I don't know if I can stand the separation," exclaimed Sasha.

Derrick said, "Sasha, you know that is the life of a dog. All we can hope for is that each one finds a loving home. Our masters know what is best for us, and we must trust them. Remember, that is a dog's life; a dog is to provide love and companionship to their owner. In return, the owner of a dog provides unconditional love to their dog. Yes, you are right, but it doesn't make it any easier. I will talk to the children," replied Derrick.

Chapter Four

Sash and Butch overheard their parents talking about the newspaper ad placed by their owner, Tammy. "They are going to sell us, and we will be taken away from the only home we have ever known."

Sash asked, "Why do you think our mother is upset?"

Butch replied, "I don't know, but let's play and have some fun. I'll chase you around the house, and I will even give you a head start."

"I don't want to play because you play too rough," said Sash.

They had no way of knowing their days were numbered here with their mom and dad.

As they were playing, there was a knock on the front door. Tammy went to the door and opened it. Standing there on the doorstep was a young woman with a brown-haired girl.

Tammy asked, "Can I help you?"

The young woman said, "Hello, my name is Faith, and this is my daughter, Sherry. I saw the ad in the newspaper, and I am here about poodles for sale. Do you still have the female poodle? We are very interested in buying the female poodle."

Tammy replied, "Yes, I still have the female poodle. Please, won't you come in? The girl poodle is called Sash, and she is running around the house with her brother. I'll go get her, and both of you can have a seat."

"Thank you very much. My daughter is anxious to see the girl poodle," replied the woman.

Tammy found Sash hiding under the dinner table. She had to coax her out from under the table. "Come on, Sash, I have someone who wants to see you," said Tammy.

Sash was thinking to herself that she didn't want to come out and meet someone new. She realized she had to mind her master.

Tammy had Sash in her arms as she entered the living room. The young girl was sitting on the couch, anxiously looking around the room.

Tammy told Sash, "I have someone here who wants to meet you." The girl was looking expectantly at the ball of fur in Tammy's arms.

The girl asked, "Can I hold her?" She was so excited that she was bursting with nervous energy.

Tammy put Sash in the girl's arms.

"Oh, she is so tiny. I love her, Mom. She can sleep in my bed, and I will take good care of her. Please, can we get her, Mom?"

Sash was shaking so hard because she was so scared. "What is happening? What does this mean? I don't want to leave my family. I want to stay here," said Sash.

Faith said, "Yes, we can get her. I brought the $200 for Sash. Is that the right amount? We will give her a good home and love her unconditionally."

"All I ask is that you take good care of her and love her," replied Tammy. "I will get her papers for you. Just give me a minute to find them."

While Tammy was gone, Sash was looking around her home for the last time. Butch was running and jumping around at their feet because he wanted to say goodbye to his sister.

Sherry lowered Sash to Butch's level so he could kiss her goodbye. Butch was licking Sash's face.

"I will always love you, sis, no matter what. You will always be my sister. Please, don't forget me," exclaimed Butch.

Sash replied, "I will never forget you, and I will always love you too."

Faith paid Tammy the money for Sash that was required. "I hate to part with Sash, but we can't afford to take her to Florida with us. All I ask is that you love her and give her a wonderful home."

Faith said, "I promise you that Sash will have a loving home. I have another daughter, and all of us will love her. We will take excellent care of her."

Tammy told her that Sash is potty trained, but moving her to a new home might cause her to have a few accidents at the beginning. She suggested using puppy pads and keeping her penned up for a while.

Faith told her that there would be no problem. Faith and Sherry headed to the car with Sash in Sherry's arms. Sash was shaking like a leaf in the autumn wind.

As they pulled out of Tammy's driveway, Sash raised to look out the window. She had big, fat teardrops rolling down her face as they pulled away from the only home she had ever known.

"What will happen to me now? Will I love my new home, and will these strangers love me? Why, oh why do I have to go? I hope and pray they will be good to me," said Sash.

Looking out the window, Sash could see the streets of the city being left behind. All new wonders assailed her senses as new scenery was met with her.

The hills and dales that they were passing through brought wonder and a sense of longing for things left behind.

Chapter Five

They finally arrived at their destination, and Sash's new home on Brown Road.

The sprawling, tan, ranch-style home stood on one and one-half acres of land in a small rural community. Two large maple trees stood like guards in the front yard. The trees had limbs reaching out as if to welcome the family home. Encompassing each maple tree were flowers blooming in a riot of color, giving off a scent as sweet as honey. An open flat field lay across from the house on Brown Road, and a crumbling antiquated stone structure stood in the far upper corner like a soldier forgotten. Houses stood in a row like soldiers in formation down one side of Brown Road. The tan house was second in line and smartly stood out from the rest.

"This is your new home, Sash. I know you will be happy here, and we will love you with all our hearts. Mom, when are we going to get Sash a bowl for her food and water?"

"We will go shortly to Walmart to get what we need for Sash, but we need to give her time to adjust to the change. Look, she is frightened."

Sash was trembling so hard that her teeth were rattling. "I am afraid, and I want to go home to my parents. I don't want to go inside the house. What am I going to do?"

Sherry gently carried Sash into the house and introduced her to her new surroundings.

Sash looked around as she entered the family room and saw a large sectional couch spread out over the room with a welcoming fireplace surrounded by red bricks. An open doorway led into a vast kitchen that was airy and open. To the left of the kitchen was a dark paneled hallway leading to a bathroom in golden yellow with black and white swirled marble flooring. Black curtains hung from the windows. At the end of the hallway, a door opened to a one-car garage with green outside carpet covering the floor.

As Sherry traced her steps back to the kitchen, she showed Sash the other rooms in the house. To the right of the kitchen was the dining room with glass-paneled patio doors leading to a large outside patio. The doorway off the dining room led to a large formal living room with soft gray carpet. The hallway led to the bedroom and master bath. Sash noticed the first bedroom on the left, which was a soft green color with light brown carpeting. Sherry told Sash that this was her room, and they would sleep in her big, soft waterbed together. The next bedroom was dark maroon with dark blue carpeting, and the last bedroom was peach in color. The master bedroom was off the master bath, which was pale ivory in color. Sherry told Sash that this was her new home and that she would soon learn her way around, and we would love her very much.

Sash looked with awe as the tour of her new home ended. "Maybe I will be happy here, but I am still so scared. I truly hope these people will love me and not hurt me."

Stacey, the oldest daughter, comes into the room wanting to see the new dog. She wanted to know if she could hold Sash. Sherry hands over the dog to her sister. Stacey holds her gently, and she thinks to herself that she is so cute and lovable.

Sash said, "I think I am going to like it here, but I am going to miss my parents and my brother, Butch. This is a dog's life to provide love and companionship to our owners.

They are supposed to love me back, and I think these three girls are going to love me to the end. I know I will be happy here."

Stacey sets Sash down on the floor so that she can explore her new home.

Sash is running around the house exploring each room. The den has light brown carpet, and the formal living room has light gray carpet. It is soft to Sash's paws and feels good to her. She rolls around on the carpet because it feels so soft to her skin.

Then she goes into each bedroom, exploring, and she thinks this sure is a big house. She runs to the dining room, and the hardwood floor feels cool to her paws, while it is hard to get traction on these floors. It is slick and very slippery. The floor in the kitchen is yellowish brown linoleum and feels cool to her paws.

Sherry took Sash to her room and showed her where she was going to sleep. Her room was light green in color with soft brown carpet. There was a twin waterbed in the room, and it was so high from the floor that Sash could not jump into it. Sherry picked her up and placed her in the waterbed. It felt so funny because it moved as she moved. It was very warm and felt so good to her. She thought to herself that she was going to love living here. Everyone loved her, which made her very happy. She thought this was going to be a wonderful home for her and that she was going to love the three girls very much.

Chapter Six

"Mom, when are we going to get Sash a bowl for her food and water?" asked Sherry.

"We will go shortly to Wal-Mart to get what we need for Sash, but we need to give her time to adjust to the change. See, she is frightened," replied Faith.

"Sash, we must put you in the bathroom until we get back with your new bowl and dog food," stated Sherry. "We won't be gone long, and you will be safe."

As the bathroom door closed, Sash wondered what to do now. "I don't like being by myself; it is all so different and new. Please let me out, and don't leave me in here."

Sash wandered around the room looking for a way out. The search was futile. "Maybe I can scratch my way out. I am going to try."

Scratch! Scratch! Scratch! "It isn't doing any good. I can't get out this way."

Sash finally lay down in the corner and curled around into a tight ball with big rolling tears falling from her eyes, dripping on the black marble floor. She couldn't understand why they left her in this room all alone.

It wasn't long until she heard a noise. "Maybe, they are back, and I can get out of this prison."

Sherry opened the door and found Sash looking up at her with big, woeful, wet eyes. "Look, Mom, Sash has been crying. I am so sorry, Sash, that we had to leave you alone, but we bought you a new bowl for food and water, along with some toys. We purchased some puppy pads in case you have an accident."

Sherry picked Sash up and gave her a loving teddy bear hug. "We also got you a collar with a bell because you are so small that we can't hear you before you are under our feet."

Faith put the collar on Sash and set her down to explore the house. Sash wandered through the rooms, and the soft tinkle could be heard as she explored her new home.

Sash thought to herself, "I believe that I am going to be very happy here. Uh-oh, I have to pee. I will go to the formal living room in the corner. Maybe no one will see me."

Sash runs to the corner and pees on the carpet.

Faith yells, "Girls, Sash is peeing on the floor."

Sherry grabs Sash and puts her outside. "Well, I guess we have a new problem. We have to teach her to go outside to pee. We will have to work together to train her girls."

www.ingramcontent.com/pod-product-compliance
Lightning Source LLC
LaVergne TN
LVHW070348090426
835513LV00026B/34